A TALE OF TWO PRINCES

published by Gold'n'Honey Books
a part of the Questar publishing family

English language edition:
© 1993 by Questar Publishers, Inc.
published in German
as *Als der Königssohn kam*
Original German edition:
© 1993 by Hänssler Verlag,
Neuhausen-Stuttgart, Germany

International Standard Book Number:
0-88070-598-1

Printed in Germany

For information:
QUESTAR PUBLISHERS, INC.
POST OFFICE BOX 1720
SISTERS, OREGON 97759

93 94 95 96 97 98 99 00 01 — 10 9 8 7 6 5 4 3 2 1

A TALE OF TWO PRINCES

Story by
ECKART ZUR NIEDEN

Illustrations by
GISELA SCHEER

English text adapted by
MACK THOMAS

Gold 'n'
Honey
BOOKS

YO HO! Come join us
for a balloon ride!
Up and up we fly,
slowly gliding in the sky,
until we discover an island....

"What a beautiful place,"
you say. And you're right—
bright-colored houses and fields,
ribbony roads and rivers,
green-gold meadows and trees,
and a lighthouse on the shore.

How many cows can we see?
And how many sheep?
How many boats,
and how many bridges?
How many swans,
and how many chickens?

AND... how many people?

Ah ha! We can't see *any* people!
No farmers, no fishermen.
No children, no mothers.
No people at all.

So you ask, "Where are they?"

Oh ho! To answer that, my friend,
I must tell you a story...

THIS LOVELY ISLAND belongs
to a king who is great and good.
Long ago, the king himself
brought many people here.
He helped them make the island beautiful.
He gave them good laws
so they knew what to do
and how to behave,
and how to always be happy.

Then the king left the island,
and traveled to his home across the sea.

The people respected the king so much
that they built a statue of him.
It stood straight and tall at the harbor-side.

And once each year,
the people loaded a ship with good things—
grain and meat from their farms,
fruit from their fruit trees,
and fish from their fishing nets.
They sent these riches across the sea,
as a gift of honor to their king.

They also chose a certain man
as their governor. His job was to help them
remember the king and his good laws.

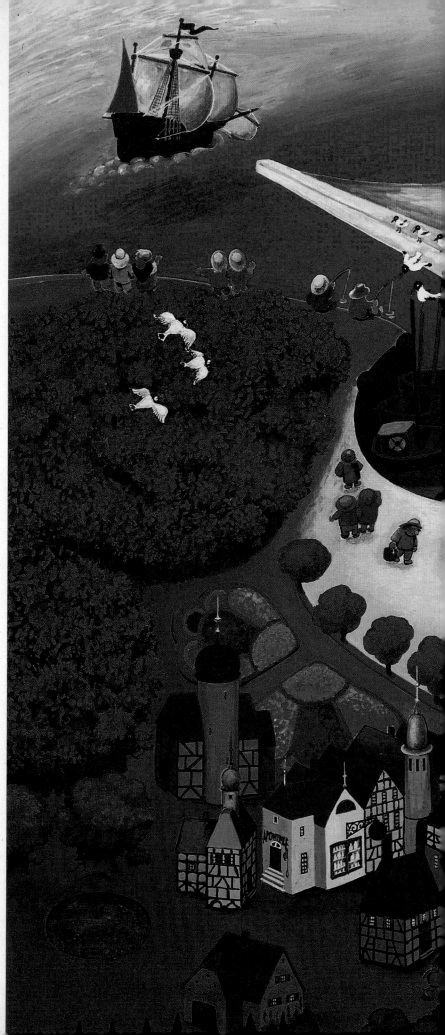

ONE DAY the governor
was walking in the forest.
He heard a deep voice
that seemed to be coming from the ground.
"Governor!" the voice called.

The governor turned to look.
But he saw no one at all.

"Governor!" the voice called again.
"I want to talk to you!
I am the prince of this island."

The governor was amazed.
"The *prince?*" he asked.

"Yes," answered the voice.
"And I have a suggestion for you."

"What kind of suggestion?"
said the governor.

"Just this," replied the voice.
"Why don't you stop honoring the king?
After all, he's so far away.
Knock down his statue!
Forget about his laws!
And don't send him that ship-load
of riches every year. Keep those good things!
Store them up for yourselves!
After all, you may need them someday
when hard times come."

The governor could hardly believe
what he was hearing. He said to the voice,
"How could we be so ungrateful
and hateful to our king?"

The voice did not answer.
So the governor walked away.
And many new thoughts
went through his head.

WHEN THE NEXT SHIP
for the king was being
loaded with riches,
the governor went down to watch.
He went early in the morning,
when sunrise made the harbor shine
like gold.

There at the harbor-side
the governor saw crates and boxes and barrels
ready to be carried aboard ship.
He also saw ten sacks of hazelnuts,
fresh from the island's hazelnut trees.

The governor stepped closer
to two of the dockworkers,
whose job it was to load the ship.
In a low voice he said to them,
"Please take two sacks of those hazelnuts
and store them in my barn.
After all, we may need them someday
when hard times come."
The dockworkers did as the governor said.

Later that day,
those dockworkers began whispering
to all the other dockworkers and sailors
who were loading the ship.
"The governor" they said,
*"is taking some of the king's riches
for HIMSELF!"*

THAT NIGHT the sailors
and dockworkers came together.
They said to each other,
"Whatever the governor can have,
we can have."

They went to the harbor-side,
and in the darkness they unloaded
all the good things from the ship.
Each man carried away some of the riches
to his own house or barn.
And some of the men took the ship
out into the ocean, and sank it.

NOW IT SO HAPPENED late that night
that a certain farmer's cow
gave birth to a new calf.

The farmer got up to check on the cow
and her baby. And what else did he see?
He saw sailors and dockworkers
taking away the king's riches!

Early the next morning
the farmer told another farmer
what he had seen.
That farmer told another farmer.
And that farmer told another.
All the farmers said to one another,
"Whatever the sailors
and dockworkers can have,
we can have!"

THE FARMERS came together
at the harbor-side,
and there someone told them
that the ship was sunk.
There were no more riches to be taken away.
The farmers were angry. In fact,
they were furious. They shouted,
"WE WANT OUR SHARE!"

Someone told the fishermen
what had happened.
That made the *fishermen* furious.
They came together and said,
"Whatever the farmers can do,
we can do!"

Then the farmers and fishermen
began storming their way into the houses
of the sailors and the dockworkers.
They took away whatever they wanted.

Now *everyone* was furious.

In all the angry confusion,
the king's statue was tipped over,
and fell with a splash into the harbor.

S O IN ONLY a night and a day,
the people of the island
had forgotten how to behave
and how to be happy.
Now they were always being hateful.
They were always scolding or complaining.
Everyone was angry, and everyone was afraid.

And no one talked about the king anymore.
And no one remembered his good laws.

ONE DAY a woman with two children
walked up to the governor.
"Look at these children," she told him.
"Now they will have to grow up in a place
where everyone is angry and afraid
and hateful and unhappy.
And it's *ALL YOUR FAULT!*"

The governor didn't agree
that this was all his fault.
"But I must do something about it,"
he decided.

HE RAN to the forest.
He found the place where
he once heard the voice
that seemed to come from the ground.

"YO HO, prince!" the governor called out.
"Say something!"

"What do you want?" answered the voice.
At once the governor told him
everything that had happened.
And he added, "It's *ALL YOUR FAULT!*
Your suggestion was terrible!"

"You can do whatever you want
with my suggestions," said the voice.
"But I know something important
that you'd better keep in mind."

"And what's that?" said the governor.

"Just this," replied the voice.
"The king has heard nothing from this island
for a long time. Surely he's angry now,
for he knows that you've forgotten him.
Very soon he'll come
and punish you all severely!"

The governor was alarmed.
"Oh, no!" he stammered. "We're lost!"

"Ohhhh, not just yet," said the voice.
"I know how you might be able
to save yourselves."

"How?" said the governor.
He trembled, and listened carefully.

"Just this," replied the voice. "Push back
those tree branches there beside you,
and you'll see a secret doorway."
The governor pushed back the branches.
He saw the opening to a cave
going deep underground.

"I'm down here," the voice said,
"in a huge cave, with plenty of room
to keep all of you safe. So run quickly
and warn the people about the danger.
Tell them about this hiding place,
and bring everyone back here with you.
Hurry! The king is coming soon!"

So the governor hurried away.
And many new thoughts
went through his head.

HE RETURNED quickly
with all the people
who lived on the island—
sailors and dockworkers,
farmers and fishermen,
mothers and children.
One after another
they followed the governor,
stepping down, down into the darkness.

The voice of the underground prince
was leading them. "This way!" he said.
"Follow me!"

Down, down, deeper and deeper they went.

After many long moments,
the governor said, "How much longer?"

"Patience, patience,"
the prince's voice answered slowly.

Down they went…deeper,
deeper into darkness.

After many more long moments,
the governor said,
"It's too dark down here. I'll strike a match."

"NO!" the prince's voice shouted.
"Don't do that! It would blind me,
and then I couldn't lead you anymore.
Besides, it's too damp down here
for a match to burn."

He was right. It *was* damp
in the deep undergound,
and it was cold,
and it was dark.

After many more long moments,
some of the children began to cry.
Some of the parents began to groan
and complain. So the governor spoke up:
"Prince, this is far enough!
We won't go a single step more!"

The prince's voice said nothing in reply.

Suddenly the governor was afraid.
"YO HO, prince! Listen to me!
Where are you?"

But again there was no answer.

THE PEOPLE didn't know it yet,
but the prince had gone back
to the cave's doorway
and sealed it shut. Now there was *no way out!*

And that, of course, was the day
our balloon glided over the island,
when we couldn't see any people down there.
They were all trapped, deep inside the cave.

So you ask,
"But please, what happened next?"

Oh ho! To answer that, my friend,
I must finish telling you the story…

SOME PEOPLE in the cave
tried to find a way out.
But no escape could be found.
So some of the children cried.
Some of the women screamed.
And some of the men growled and howled.
But of course, none of that helped.

"Hush, everyone!" the governor ordered.
"Calm down!"

They were all quiet for a moment.
Then from somewhere in the darkness,
they heard a laugh. It sounded
like the voice of the underground prince.

"Where are you?" the governor demanded.

"You can't see me," the voice said,
"But I can see you."

The governor raised his fists.
"You cheated us!" he said.
"You lied to us!
Who are you, anyway?"

"I will tell you only this," said the voice:
"Long ago I lived across the sea
in the king's home, which is bright
and full of light. One day I told him
that I wanted to be king instead of him.
I attacked him and fought him fiercely,
but he defeated me. He threw me out
of his home. So across the sea I came,
to make myself prince of this island.
Now I hate the light, and I love darkness.
Maybe you will learn to love it too…
for I will never let you out of here!"

He laughed again; then all was silent.
Has he gone away? the people wondered.
*Or is he still staring at us
from the cold darkness?*

S AD AND AFRAID,
the people crowded together
to comfort one another,
and to keep each other warm.

A long time passed.
And no one ever knew if it was day or night,
for here in the cave there was only darkness.

The people were tired, and tried to sleep.
But now and then a child would cry.
Now and then a woman would scream
from a terrible dream. And now and then
a man would growl or howl.

Of course, none of that helped.

And there in the cold, damp darkness,
the people began to feel sorry
for the wrong things they had done.

T HEN CAME the moment
when someone whispered:
"I see a light!"

"Where?"

"There! Look!"

Yes, it was true—far away was a glowing light.
Everyone stared as the brightness came closer.

Suddenly it stopped.
Everyone heard the sound of fighting—
groans and shouts,
and the clash and clang of weapons.
The light jerked this way and that.

Finally the battle sounds ended.
Slowly the light came forward again,
closer and closer. Soon the people could see
the shadow of a man carrying a torch.
He was staggering and limping,
as if he had been hurt.

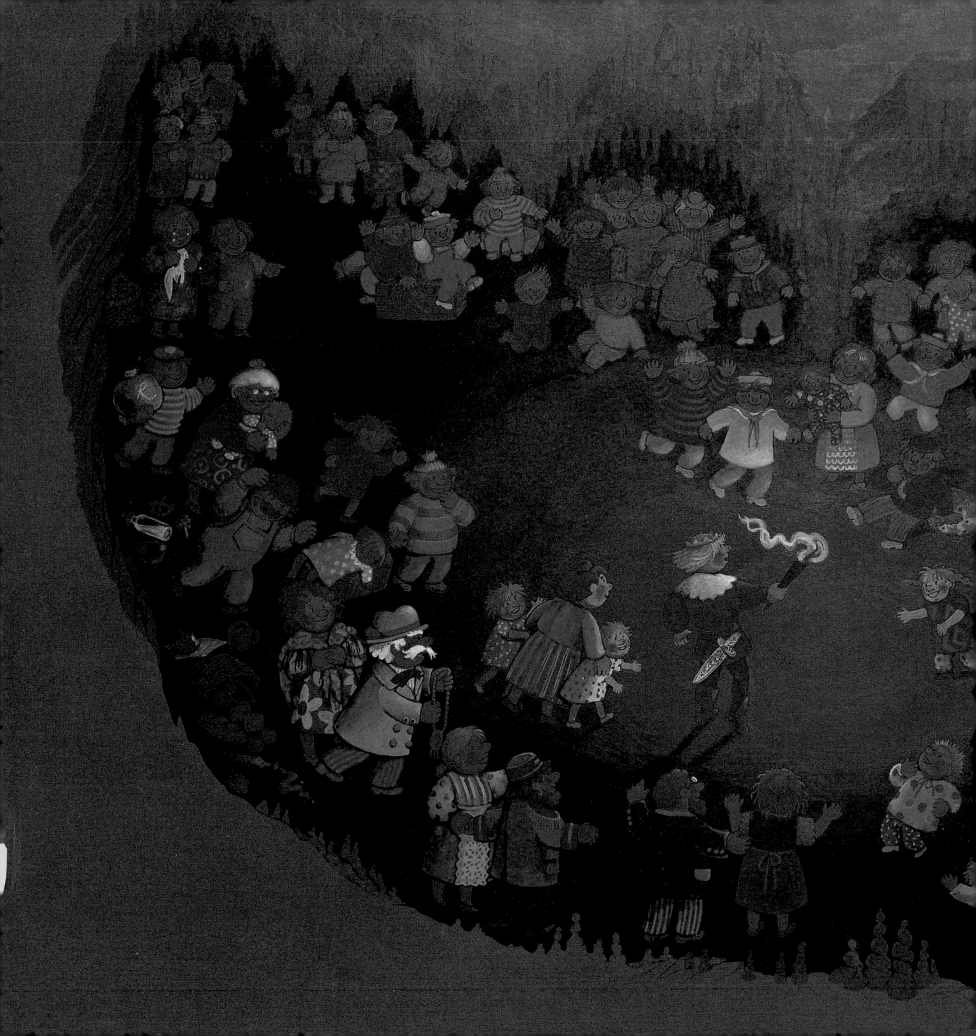

THE MAN came and stood in front of everyone, in the bright circle made by his torch-light.

Those in front could see
that his heel was bleeding.

"Don't be afraid," the man said to everyone.
"I've come to take you out of this place.
I am the king's son."

The king's son! The people
were astonished, and fearful at first.

"Don't be afraid," the king's son said again.
"My father forgives all of you
for all the wrong things you did.
I've found you now, and you are safe,
and you can follow me home…"

"But—but the prince!" said the governor.
"The underground prince—"

"He is defeated," said the king's son
in a quiet, sure voice. "He attacked me,
but I overcame him, and he can never
keep you in the darkness again.
So come; follow me!"

Holding each other's hands, the people
followed the king's son on the long trip up
and out of the cave…and into the warmth
and brightness above.

THAT EVENING, the king's son
went aboard his ship
to return to his father's home
across the sea. "But someday
I'll come back," he promised the people.

With waves and cheers and tears,
the people watched his ship sail away.

As it went out to sea,
the ship looked smaller and smaller
and smaller. Finally it disappeared
from their sight.

AND STILL TODAY,
this is what happens
on the beautiful island:
Sailors and dockworkers
and farmers and fishermen
and mothers and children
go often to an open window
or upon a high hill
or to the lighthouse on the shore.
There they gaze out across the sea—
and remember the king's son…

and wait for his return.